T0179775

to:

....

from:

....

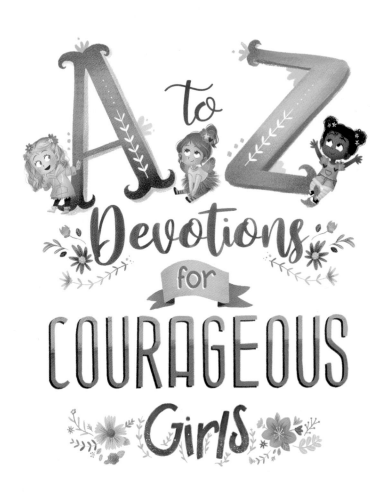

A to Z Devotions for Courageous Girls

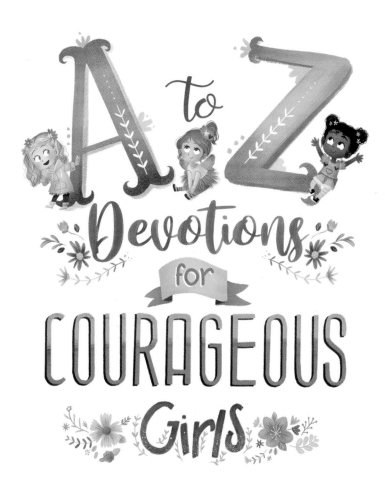

A to Z Devotions for COURAGEOUS Girls

KELLY MCINTOSH

BARBOUR **kidz**

A Division of Barbour Publishing

Published by Barbour Publishing, Inc., 1810 Barbour Drive, Uhrichsville, Ohio 44683, www.barbourbooks.com.

Our mission is to inspire the world with the life-changing message of the Bible.

Member of the
Evangelical Christian
Publishers Association

Printed in China.
002205   1024   XY

COURAGEOUS GIRLS ARE...

*"Let the little children
come to Me. Do not stop them.
The holy nation of God is made
up of ones like these."*

MARK 10:14

YOU ARE GOD'S COURAGEOUS GIRL!

What does it take to be a courageous girl of God?

You'll find out in this fun devotional
book created especially for you.

Each reading touches on a
positive character trait—from A to Z!

Are you **A**dventurous?...

What about **G**enerous and **K**ind?...

Or **P**atient and **W**ise?...

With each turn of the page, you'll be inspired
to grow up God's way and become the wonderfully
courageous girl He created you to be!

When you decide to follow Jesus, life is always full of adventure.

He might ask you to do something new—and maybe that "something new" will make you feel a little nervous (like butterflies in your tummy). He might want you to share something about Him with a neighbor. Or He might even ask you to volunteer your free time at church. Or maybe even go on a mission trip—near your home state or far, far away.

Whatever it is, you can be sure that when you say *yes* to Jesus, you'll be so glad you did. His way is *always* best!

THINK ABOUT IT:

What is something adventurous God might ask you to do?

You will show me the way of life.
Being with You is to be full of joy.
In Your right hand there is happiness forever.
PSALM 16:11

Courageous girls are Brave!

*D*id you know that being brave means facing your fears with courage? *Courage* is when you have a strong mind and determination. It doesn't mean you're *never* afraid of anything.

The truth is, everyone is afraid of something. Think about it: What are you most afraid of?...And when you are afraid, how do you deal with it?

Whether you're afraid of the dark or thunderstorms or creepy-crawly bugs...if you ask God to help you face your fears with courage, He'll hear you, and He'll help calm your worried heart.

THINK ABOUT IT:

When do you feel the most brave?

"Be strong and have strength of heart. Do not be afraid or shake with fear because of them. For the Lord your God is the One Who goes with you. He will be faithful to you. He will not leave you alone."

DEUTERONOMY 31:6

Courageous girls are Confident!

*A*re you confident? To answer this question, you need to know what *confident* means.

Being *confident* means that you're sure of yourself—you don't wonder whether you're good enough...or smart enough...or talented enough. You *know* you're perfect just the way God made you.

If you ever begin to worry or wonder—if you ever feel unsure of yourself—talk to God and read His Word. He'll remind you that *you are His*. And that's all the confidence a girl could ever need!

THINK ABOUT IT:
**What things could you say or
do to help a friend feel confident?**

*Let us go with complete trust to the throne of God.
We will receive His loving-kindness and have
His loving-favor to help us whenever we need it.*

HEBREWS 4:16

Courageous girls are Dependable!

When Mom or Dad asks you to do something, do they know they can count on you? Do you say, "Yes," and then do it? Or do you say, "Sure, I'll do it later"...and then forget all about it?

Courageous girls of God shine their lights for Him when they are dependable. Following through on a request from your parents honors them—and it sets a great example for your brothers, sisters, and your friends too!

The next time you're given an opportunity to be dependable, say, "Yes!"

THINK ABOUT IT:

Share about a time when you showed that you were dependable. How did it make you feel?

There are many people who belong to Christ.
And yet, we are one body which is Christ's.
We are all different but we depend on each other.
ROMANS 12:5

Courageous girls are
Encouraging!

What can you do if a friend is going through something super hard or just having a terrible, horrible day? While you might not be able to fix your friends' problems for them, you can do something to help...

You can be an *encourager*!

Encouragers do many things to give others hope and support when they need it most. Showing you care doesn't have to be difficult. You can encourage others with simple things like kind words, handwritten notes, small gifts, or hugs.

Do you know someone who could use some encouraging today? Show you care with a kind word or action, and then lift them in prayer!

THINK ABOUT IT:

Can you think of other ways to offer encouragement to someone who needs it?

Remember to do good and help each other. Gifts like this please God.
HEBREWS 13:16

Courageous girls are
Forgiving!

Has a friend ever hurt your feelings? If so, how did it make you feel? Were you sad or angry?

When friends do or say hurtful things, it's hard to forgive them. But God wants us to show His love by offering forgiveness and then moving on. This is just what He does for us when we make a mistake…He forgives us *no matter what we've done*. And still, He loves us!

Today ask God to help you say, "You're forgiven." If mighty God can erase mistakes from His mind, we can too!

THINK ABOUT IT:
Why is it so hard to forgive?
Why is it important to forgive?

You must be kind to each other.
Think of the other person. Forgive
other people just as God forgave you.
EPHESIANS 4:32

Courageous girls are
Generous!

id you know that the Bible says God loves people who give because they *want* to give? It also says that the way you give will be the same way you get. What that means is the more you give to others, the more you'll be blessed.

Courageous girls are generous givers. This means they give *more* of what they have. They don't give just a little bit. They give *a lot*!

Ask God to give you the energy you need to keep being generous. The more you focus on giving to others, the happier you'll be!

THINK ABOUT IT:

In what ways can you be more generous?

"Give, and it will be given to you. You will have more than enough. It can be pushed down and shaken together and it will still run over as it is given to you. The way you give to others is the way you will receive in return."

LUKE 6:38

Courageous girls
are **Honest!**

Is it ever okay to tell a lie? . . . Even a "little" one?

Telling the truth can be really hard sometimes, especially if it means we'll probably get into trouble for something we shouldn't have done in the first place.

But lies—even little ones—almost always lead to more trouble and even more lies. And before you know it, you have one big mess that hurts you and others. So what's a girl to do?

Follow God and His Word: be honest! It's important to God. It's what He expects from His courageous girls!

THINK ABOUT IT:

Have you ever told a lie and wished you could take it back? What would have been different if you had told the truth instead?

All the words of my mouth are right and good.
There is nothing in them that is against the truth.
PROVERBS 8:8

Courageous girls are
Inspiring!

*D*id you know that when you follow Jesus and make good choices for your life, you inspire others to do the same? It's true! A girl who follows Jesus and does her very best to obey Him sets a great example for others to follow.

Others will notice how you live your life. Just think about all the adults and kids you know who've watched how you talk and act. When they see your life is different—and *good!*—they'll wonder how they can have a good life too!...

And then you can tell them all about Jesus! There's nothing better than that!

THINK ABOUT IT:

If someone asks, are you ready to tell him or her about Jesus? What would you say?

Let us keep looking to Jesus. Our faith comes from Him and He is the One Who makes it perfect.
HEBREWS 12:2

It's easy to be happy and joyful when everything is going your way.

But what about when life is hard?

Mom and Dad say no when you really, really, *really* wanted them to say yes.
Your favorite toy gets broken or lost.
You have an argument with your brother or sister or your best friend.

It might seem impossible, but the truth is, with God, you can feel joyful even when everything isn't as you hoped it would be.

Ask God to give you joy—even in the middle of the not-so-good stuff—and He will answer your prayer!

THINK ABOUT IT:

When is it hard to feel joyful, and what can you do to help turn your feelings around?

But I have trusted in Your loving-kindness.
My heart will be full of joy because You will save me.
Psalm 13:5

Courageous girls are
Kind!

When someone is kind to you, how does it make you feel? You probably feel happy and loved. . .and you might even have the warm fuzzies inside!

When Jesus was here on earth, He was the perfect example of kindness. He made people feel loved and important. He helped people who were poor, sick, or in pain. If you read the Bible, you'll see again and again, that Jesus showed kindness to *all* people.

His example is one that courageous girls should follow. Show kindness to all people. . .no matter what they look like. . .no matter where they come from. . .and you'll shine your light for Jesus!

THINK ABOUT IT:

Why is it sometimes hard to be kind? Why is it so important to be kind to all people?

Be gentle and kind. Do not be hard on others.
Let love keep you from doing that.
EPHESIANS 4:2

Courageous girls are Loyal!

When you really believe in someone or something and don't keep changing your mind about it, that's loyalty!

You can be loyal to a friend or family member, a church or sports team. . .and you can be loyal to God!

If you're loyal to God, it means you believe in Him and His Word with all your heart. You know that, no matter what, He is on your side. He loves you, and you love Him. And you'll follow Him forever.

God wants His courageous girls to be loyal!

THINK ABOUT IT:

How can you show loyalty to a friend or family member? How can you show loyalty to God?

[The person] who follows what is right and loving and kind finds life, right-standing with God and honor.
PROVERBS 21:21

M

Courageous girls are

Mannerly!

"Please."
"Thank you."
"Excuse me."
"Yes, Ma'am." "Yes, Sir."
"No, Ma'am." "No, Sir."

If you're wondering what all these phrases have in common, it's this: when you say them, it shows you have manners!

And when you have manners, it shows that you are considerate, or thoughtful of the needs and feelings of others.

If you want to shine your light for Jesus, manners really matter. When you're polite, other people will notice your good example. They'll want to know what makes you so different.

What makes you stand out, courageous girl? JESUS!

THINK ABOUT IT:

Your manners matter in how you talk, but they also matter in the things you do. Can you name some ways your actions can show you have manners too?

Let the words of my mouth and the thoughts of my heart be pleasing in Your eyes, O Lord, my Rock and the One Who saves me.

PSALM 19:14

Courageous girls are Nice!

What does it mean to be nice?
Does it mean that you say kind things?
Does it mean that you're friendly?
Does it mean that you're helpful?
Does it mean that you share with others?
Being nice is all these things and more.

When you're nice, other people want to be around you. They want to spend time with you, because it's fun to be around people who are nice!

And even better, when you're nice, it makes other kids want to be nice too!

Spread some niceness around you today, courageous girl!

THINK ABOUT IT:

Why is it important to be nice?

*"Do for other people whatever you
would like to have them do for you."*
MATTHEW 7:12

*D*o you *always* do what you're told? When Mom or Dad asks for your help, do you say "Sure!" with a smile on your face? Or do you grump and groan, scowl and pout? . . .

There's a Sunday school song that says, "Obedience is the very best way to show that you believe." This means the best way to show that you follow Jesus is to follow His Word and do what it says. And God's Word says that it's important for kids to obey their parents.

So the next time Mom or Dad needs your help, say *yes!* Even better, say it with a smile!

THINK ABOUT IT:

Why is learning to be obedient so important? When you're obedient, how does that make your mom, dad, and God feel?

Children, as Christians, obey your parents. This is the right thing to do. Respect your father and mother.
EPHESIANS 6:1–2

Courageous girls are
Patient!

ave you ever had to wait. . .and wait. . .and *wait* for something?

How did it make you feel? . . . Frustrated? Angry? Worried? Nervous?

Whether you're looking forward to a family vacation, waiting for your parents to answer *yes* or *no*, expecting your friend to hurry up and give you a turn, or stuck in a slow-moving line at school. . .waiting quietly and calmly without complaining is *so very hard.*

But God's Word tells us we should be patient. And God always knows best. Ask Him for His help while you wait.

THINK ABOUT IT:

What are some things you might do while you're waiting to help you be more patient?

Since God chose you to be the holy people he loves, you must clothe yourselves with tenderhearted mercy, kindness, humility, gentleness, and patience.

Colossians 3:12 NLT

Courageous girls are
Quiet!

*D*id you know that being quiet doesn't just mean you aren't loud?

It doesn't mean you only speak in a whisper. . .or that you never yell on the playground. . .or that you don't giggle too loudly when your friend tells a joke. God is okay with all those things.

Being quiet can also mean you have peace on the inside. You are calm. You aren't worried and ruffled up.

This kind of quiet happens when you have Jesus in your heart. He will take all your worry and twisted-up feelings and give you peace. Ask Him to give you quiet today.

THINK ABOUT IT:

Why does God want us to be quiet on the inside?

A heart that has peace is life to the body.
PROVERBS 14:30

Courageous girls are
Responsible!

o you help Mom or Dad with chores at home? Can they always count on you to do what you're asked?

Do you feed your pet?

Do you keep your room clean?

Do you help set the table and clean up after dinner?

If so, you're showing responsibility!

Being responsible takes hard work. There will always be days when you'd rather *not* do what Mom or Dad asks you to do.

But if you remember that God's Word says we should do all of our work like we're doing it for Him and not other people—not for Mom or Dad, not for a teacher, not for a brother or sister—doesn't that make you want to be responsible every day of the week?

THINK ABOUT IT:

Do you think you're responsible? Why or why not?

Whatever work you do, do it with all your heart.
Do it for the Lord and not for men.
Colossians 3:23

If someone has big muscles, how would you describe that person? You'd probably say he or she is strong, right?

There's another kind of strong that doesn't have anything to do with big muscles—this different kind of strength comes from knowing and trusting God.

When you're nervous or worried, sad or afraid, you can ask God to make you strong. His Word—the Bible—promises that He will make you strong and give you the courage you need to get through any situation. And even better. . .when God makes a promise, He keeps it!

THINK ABOUT IT:

Are you nervous, worried, sad, or afraid about anything today? What can you do to get the kind of strength described in today's devotional reading?

You answered me on the day I called.
You gave me strength in my soul.
PSALM 138:3

Have you ever had a *really* bad day? The kind of day when nothing seemed to go your way—from the time you opened your sleepy eyes in the morning until you closed your tired eyes at night?...

Everyone has bad days sometimes. But the good news is that you *can* control how you react—it's even possible to turn a bad day into a thankful kind of day.

The next time you have a bad day, think about what's good in your life—your wonderful family, your cuddly pet, your best friend...and thank God for all the things He's given you to enjoy!

THINK ABOUT IT:

**Name all the good things God has given you.
Then say a prayer of thanks to God!**

Always give thanks for all things to God the Father in the name of our Lord Jesus Christ.
Ephesians 5:20

Courageous girls are Unique!

When you look in a mirror, what do you see?...
Do you see a nose sprinkled with freckles or a headful of crazy curls? Ocean-blue eyes or root beer brown... or maybe even sparkling green?

Whatever it is that you see, God chose it *especially* for you! He chose *everything* about you when He created you! He made you to be unique—to be different from everyone else.

The next time you look in the mirror, thank God for the fine job He did making you, His courageous girl!

THINK ABOUT IT:

What things about you make you stand out from everyone else on the planet?

For You made the parts inside me. You put me together inside my mother. I will give thanks to You, for the greatness of the way I was made.... Your works are great and my soul knows it very well.
PSALM 139:13–14

Virtuous is a very big word that means "good." Virtuous girls make good choices, set a good example, and treat others well. They are interested in always doing the right thing. . .even when it's hard.

Sound impossible? With God's help, it isn't.

If you read the Bible and do what God says, being virtuous is *always* possible. Just ask for His help. He will give you the strength you need to make the right choices— every time.

THINK ABOUT IT:
When is it hard to do the right thing?

She opens her mouth with wisdom.
The teaching of kindness is on her tongue.
PROVERBS 31:26

Courageous girls are
Wise!

If you're wise, does that mean you're super-duper smart? Or does it mean something else?

Being wise doesn't mean you get the best grades in school or that you can name all the bones in the human body. Nope!

If a girl has wisdom, she thinks about things first, *before* she takes action. She doesn't make a decision quickly. A wise girl wants to be sure she's making a good choice.

There's only one place you can get wisdom, and it isn't found in a book. It comes from God Himself.

Ask Him to give you wisdom today!

THINK ABOUT IT:

How can you be sure you're making a wise decision?

If you do not have wisdom, ask God for it.
He is always ready to give it to you.
JAMES 1:5

*C*ourageous girls of God stand out in the world. This means they're extraordinary!

Being extraordinary doesn't mean that you're rich. It doesn't mean you're famous. It doesn't mean you have the most friends. It doesn't mean you're the most talented.

Being *extraordinary* means that you make a difference in the world around you. You help to make the world a better place.

When you follow Jesus, there are so many things you can do to make a difference.... Pray for your friends, family, and neighbors. Serve at church. Share God's love with someone who needs it. Be kind. Be a good example.

With God's help, you can lead an extraordinary life!

THINK ABOUT IT:

How can you make a difference in the world?

"If your whole body is full of light, with no dark part, then it will shine. It will be as a lamp that gives light."
LUKE 11:36

Courageous girls are
Young!

*H*ave you ever heard someone say, "You can't! You're too young"?

While you aren't all grown up yet, God's Word says that you *can* work for Him...no matter how young you are! Isn't that exciting?

What kind of work can you do for God? You can set an example for others of how to live. This means that you choose your words carefully and make sure what you say honors God. It also means that you show love to others in the things you do and the way you treat them.

When you make the right choices, others will learn from you and see the best way to live! What a wonderful job for a young, courageous girl!

THINK ABOUT IT:

What are some other ways you can work for God?

Let no one show little respect for you because you are young.
Show other Christians how to live by your life. They should
be able to follow you in the way you talk and in what you do.
Show them how to live in faith and in love and in holy living.
1 TIMOTHY 4:12

Zippy is a funny word that means "full of energy." And followers of Jesus should always be zippy—especially when it comes to their faith in God.

When you have Jesus in your heart, it's your job to show others how wonderful that is. And when you're full of happy energy at church, at home, in school, and in your neighborhood, others will wonder why you're so full of life—and they'll want that same kind of feeling in their lives too.

Today you can be a great example for others who might not know Jesus or for kids who are just getting to know Him. Share that zippy personality, courageous girl!

THINK ABOUT IT:

In what ways are you zippy—and how can that inspire others to follow Jesus too?

But they who wait upon the Lord will get new strength. They will rise up with wings like eagles. They will run and not get tired. They will walk and not become weak.
ISAIAH 40:31

MORE ENCOURAGEMENT
FOR COURAGEOUS GIRLS LIKE YOU!

100 EXTRAORDINARY STORIES FOR COURAGEOUS GIRLS

Girls are world-changers! And this deeply inspiring storybook proves it! This collection of 100 extraordinary stories of women of faith—from the Bible, history, and today—will empower you to know and understand how women have made a difference in the world and how much smaller our faith (and the biblical record) would be without them.

Paperback / 978-1-63609-998-9